Exploring the Complexities of Mother-in-Law, Daughter-in-Law Relationships

C. P. Kumar
Reiki Healer
Roorkee - 247667, India

Disclaimer

While every effort has been made to ensure the accuracy and completeness of the content in this book, the author cannot guarantee that the information contained herein is error-free, up-to-date, or suitable for every individual circumstance.

The author shall not be held liable or responsible for any errors or omissions in the content of the book, nor for any damages, or losses that may arise from any actions taken based upon the suggestions or contents presented in the book.

Readers are advised to use their own judgment and discretion in applying the information provided in this book, and to consult with qualified professionals before taking any action based on the contents of this book. The author disclaims any and all liability or responsibility for any actions taken or not taken based on the information contained in this book.

DEDICATION

This book is dedicated to the complexities, challenges, and beauty of your relationship. It is a testament to the intricate dance you engage in, the delicate balance you strive to achieve, and the transformative potential within your connection.

To the mothers-in-law who have welcomed new daughters into their families, embracing them with open arms and nurturing them as their own. Your wisdom, love, and guidance shape the foundations of this relationship, and your unconditional support is a beacon of strength.

To the daughters-in-law who have entered unfamiliar territories, navigating the uncharted waters of becoming part of a new family. Your resilience, adaptability, and desire to build bridges of understanding are invaluable, as you bring new perspectives and diversity to the tapestry of this relationship.

This book serves as a tribute to the complexities that arise within the mother-in-law and daughter-in-law relationship. Through the exploration of its dynamics, historical influences, and the impact of expectations and stereotypes, we aim to shed light on the intricacies that shape your interactions.

It is a homage to the importance of recognizing individual personalities, understanding the challenges of communication, and unraveling the power struggles that may arise. By delving into the significance of emotional boundaries, the clashes of traditions and values, and the role of the husband as a mediator, we strive to provide insights that foster empathy, respect, and harmony.

This dedication is an acknowledgement of the emotional support that both mothers-in-law and daughters-in-law require in their journey. It recognizes the need for effective conflict resolution strategies, the development of mutual respect, and the reinforcement of positive interactions to sustain a healthy and fulfilling relationship.

To those seeking guidance and understanding, we offer practical tips and strategies to cultivate long-term harmony. By emphasizing personal growth, self-reflection, and the establishment of healthy boundaries, we hope to empower you with the tools needed to navigate the intricacies of this relationship with grace and compassion.

May this book serve as a compass, guiding you through the complexities of the mother-in-law and daughter-in-law relationship, and may it inspire deeper connections, mutual respect, and lasting harmony in your lives.

With heartfelt gratitude and admiration,

C. P. Kumar

CONTENTS

PREFACE

The relationship between a mother-in-law and daughter-in-law is a unique and intricate bond that has captivated societies across cultures and generations. It is a dynamic filled with love, shared experiences, and, at times, complexities that can challenge even the strongest familial ties. Exploring the depths of this relationship and unraveling its complexities is the aim of this book.

"Exploring the Complexities of Mother-in-Law, Daughter-in-Law Relationships" delves into the multifaceted nature of this bond, shedding light on the various factors that influence its dynamics. Through an in-depth exploration of historical perspectives, cultural influences, and societal expectations, we strive to understand the roots of this intricate relationship.

Each chapter in this book addresses a crucial aspect of the mother-in-law and daughter-in-law relationship, highlighting the challenges and opportunities for growth that arise within. We dissect preconceived notions and stereotypes associated with in-law relationships, exposing the misconceptions that can hinder genuine connection and mutual understanding.

Recognizing the role of individual personalities in shaping interactions, we examine how different temperaments and perspectives can impact the dynamics of this relationship. Moreover, we delve into the communication challenges that often arise, providing insights and strategies to foster effective dialogue and mitigate misunderstandings.

Power struggles, stemming from perceived authority and control, are explored, revealing the underlying conflicts that can strain the relationship. The importance of establishing emotional boundaries is emphasized, as we recognize the significance of preserving one's autonomy and emotional well-being.

Traditions, values, and beliefs can clash, creating further tension in this intricate relationship. We navigate the complexities of these clashes, offering guidance on how to find common ground while respecting the uniqueness of each family's heritage.

Acknowledging the pivotal role of the husband as a mediator, we shed light on the challenges he faces in balancing the needs and expectations of both his mother and wife. The importance of emotional support and understanding from all parties involved is emphasized, recognizing that empathy and compassion are vital ingredients for nurturing healthy relationships.

Conflict resolution strategies are provided to equip readers with practical tools for effectively managing disputes and fostering reconciliation. We explore techniques to develop empathy and understanding, encouraging personal growth and self-reflection for improved relationships.

Mutual respect is the cornerstone of any harmonious relationship, and we delve into its significance in the mother-in-law and daughter-in-law bond. By appreciating and respecting each other's perspectives and choices, we can bridge the gaps that divide and foster genuine connections.

Fostering positive interactions is essential in cultivating a nurturing environment for this relationship to flourish. We highlight the importance of cherishing and reinforcing positive moments, creating a solid foundation of trust and goodwill.

Setting healthy boundaries is vital for all parties involved, and we provide guidance on how to establish boundaries that promote respect and harmony. We also discuss the potential benefits of seeking professional mediation in resolving complex issues that may arise.

Personal growth and self-reflection are encouraged throughout the book, as we believe that cultivating a deeper understanding of oneself is key to fostering healthier connections with others. By embarking on this journey of self-discovery, readers can navigate the intricacies of the mother-in-law and daughter-in-law relationship with newfound wisdom and clarity.

Ultimately, "Exploring the Complexities of Mother-in-Law, Daughter-in-Law Relationships" aims to provide practical tips and strategies for sustaining healthy relationships in the long term. By embracing empathy, understanding, and open communication, readers can embark on a journey of growth and create harmonious bonds that transcend societal expectations and cultural boundaries.

As we embark on this exploration together, let us dive deep into the complexities of the mother-in-law and daughter-in-law relationship, fostering connections that transcend generations and create a lasting legacy of love and understanding.

C. P. Kumar
Reiki Healer
E-mail: cpkumar@yahoo.com
Web: https://www.angelfire.com/nh/cpkumar/virgo.html

Introduction

The relationship between a mother-in-law and daughter-in-law is often portrayed in popular culture as one fraught with tension and conflict. This complex dynamic has been a subject of fascination and curiosity for generations, fueling countless jokes, anecdotes, and even sitcoms. However, beneath the stereotypes and generalizations, lies a rich and nuanced relationship that can be both rewarding and challenging. In this article, we delve into the complexities of the mother-in-law and daughter-in-law relationship, shedding light on its dynamics, potential sources of conflict, and strategies for building a harmonious bond.

Historical and Cultural Context

To understand the dynamics of the mother-in-law and daughter-in-law relationship, it is crucial to consider the historical and cultural context that shapes their interactions. Throughout history, marriage has often marked a significant transition for women, as they leave their natal families to join their husbands' households. This shift in roles and responsibilities can lead to power struggles and an inherent sense of competition between the two women involved.

In many cultures, societal expectations and gender roles further complicate this relationship. Traditional gender norms may assign the role of the primary caregiver to the mother-in-law, causing conflicts when the daughter-in-law attempts to assert her own parenting style. Cultural differences, such as language barriers, customs, and traditions, can also contribute to misunderstandings and tensions.

Challenges and Sources of Conflict

Unrealistic Expectations: Both the mother-in-law and daughter-in-law often enter the relationship with preconceived notions and expectations. The mother-in-law may have envisioned a certain role for herself as the matriarch of the family, while the daughter-in-law may have her own ideas about her independence and autonomy. These differing expectations can lead to disappointment and resentment.

Communication Breakdowns: Effective communication is essential in any relationship, but it becomes particularly crucial in the mother-in-law and daughter-in-law dynamic. Misunderstandings, assumptions, and lack of clarity can result in conflicts and strained relations. Differences in communication styles, influenced by generational and cultural factors, can exacerbate the problem.

Boundaries and Autonomy: Issues related to boundaries and autonomy can be a significant source of tension in this relationship. The mother-in-law may feel a sense of entitlement or interference, while the daughter-in-law may perceive the mother-in-law's involvement as intrusive. Balancing the need for support and respect for personal space is vital for a healthy relationship.

Loyalty and Prioritization: A common challenge faced by both parties is navigating loyalty and prioritization. The husband, who is the son to the mother-in-law and spouse to the daughter-in-law, often finds himself caught in the middle. The daughter-in-law may feel her needs are not prioritized, while the mother-in-law may fear losing her son's affection and attention.

Building a Harmonious Relationship

Open and Honest Communication: Clear and respectful communication is crucial for building understanding and resolving conflicts. Both the mother-in-law and daughter-in-law should express their feelings, concerns, and expectations openly, while actively listening to each other's perspectives. Avoiding assumptions and embracing empathy can help foster a healthy dialogue.

Setting Boundaries: Establishing and respecting boundaries is essential for creating a balanced relationship. Both parties should communicate their needs and expectations regarding personal space, decision-making, and involvement in each other's lives. Recognizing and accepting each other's individuality can pave the way for a more harmonious connection.

Empathy and Understanding: Cultivating empathy and seeking to understand each other's perspectives is crucial for bridging the gap between generations and cultures. Acknowledging the unique challenges faced by both the mother-in-law and daughter-in-law can help foster compassion and patience. This understanding can promote a more supportive and inclusive environment.

Finding Common Ground: Identifying shared interests and activities can serve as a foundation for bonding and building a positive relationship. Engaging in shared hobbies, attending family events together, or simply spending quality time can help create meaningful connections and strengthen the bond between the two women.

Conclusion

The mother-in-law and daughter-in-law relationship is a complex and multifaceted bond that has been subject to various stereotypes and generalizations. However, understanding the dynamics and challenges inherent in this relationship can help pave the way for a more harmonious connection. By embracing open communication, setting boundaries, practicing empathy, and finding common ground, both parties can navigate the complexities and build a strong, supportive relationship that benefits the entire family. Ultimately, it is through mutual respect, understanding, and love that the mother-in-law and daughter-in-law can forge a lasting and meaningful bond.

Introduction

The relationship between a mother-in-law and a daughter-in-law is a complex interplay of emotions, expectations, and dynamics. Throughout history, this relationship has been influenced by various cultural and societal factors, shaping the attitudes and behaviors of both parties involved. Understanding the historical perspectives of the mother-in-law, daughter-in-law relationship is crucial for appreciating the complexities that arise within this familial bond. In this article, we will delve into the historical background and shed light on how cultural and societal influences have shaped this intricate relationship over time. By examining different cultural contexts, we can gain a deeper understanding of the challenges and opportunities that arise within these relationships.

Ancient Societies

In ancient societies, the mother-in-law, daughter-in-law relationship often had significant implications for family structures and social dynamics. In many cultures, the mother-in-law held a position of authority and power, serving as the matriarch of the household. Her role involved imparting wisdom, maintaining family traditions, and ensuring the continuity of the lineage. The daughter-in-law, on the other hand, was expected to conform to the established norms and customs of her new family.

For example, in ancient China, Confucian values emphasized filial piety and hierarchical family structures. The mother-in-law played a dominant role, and the daughter-in-law was expected to demonstrate respect and obedience. Similarly, in ancient India, the mother-in-law assumed a position of authority, and the daughter-in-law's primary duty was to support her husband and his family. These ancient cultural norms heavily influenced the dynamics and expectations within the mother-in-law, daughter-in-law relationship.

Middle Ages and Renaissance

During the Middle Ages (5th century to the 14th century) and Renaissance (14th century to the 17th century), the mother-in-law, daughter-in-law relationship continued to evolve within the framework of societal changes. The influence of religion and the rise of patriarchy played significant roles in shaping these dynamics. In Western societies, women were often seen as subordinate to men and were expected to adhere to strict gender roles.

In this era, the mother-in-law's position became more tenuous, as the husband became the primary authority figure in the household. The daughter-in-law, while still expected to demonstrate respect, also faced pressure to bear children and ensure the family's lineage. The mother-in-law often acted as a mediator between her son and daughter-in-law, striving to maintain harmony within the family unit.

Modern Times

The mother-in-law, daughter-in-law relationship in modern times reflects the changing dynamics of society. As women gained more autonomy and equality, the dynamics within the family structure also shifted. The traditional hierarchy and rigid expectations of the past have given way to more flexible and egalitarian relationships.

In many cultures, the mother-in-law, daughter-in-law relationship has become more inclusive, with an emphasis on mutual respect and understanding. Women now have greater agency in shaping their own lives, and the mother-in-law, daughter-in-law relationship is increasingly seen as a partnership rather than a hierarchical structure.

However, challenges persist. Cultural differences, conflicting expectations, and generational gaps can still strain these relationships. Issues such as boundary-setting, communication, and power dynamics may arise, requiring open dialogue and a willingness to navigate these complexities.

Conclusion

The mother-in-law, daughter-in-law relationship has a rich history influenced by cultural and societal norms. From ancient societies to modern times, the roles, expectations, and dynamics within this relationship have evolved significantly. Understanding the historical perspectives allows us to appreciate the complexities that arise in these familial bonds and sheds light on the challenges faced by both parties.

While historical influences have shaped the mother-in-law, daughter-in-law relationship, it is essential to recognize that contemporary relationships are also shaped by individual personalities, experiences, and societal changes. Navigating these relationships requires empathy, effective communication, and a willingness to adapt to new circumstances.

Exploring the historical context of the mother-in-law, daughter-in-law relationship helps us recognize the progress made in challenging traditional gender roles and hierarchies. By acknowledging the impact of cultural and societal influences, we can strive for more harmonious and supportive relationships within our families. Ultimately, understanding the historical perspectives of this relationship allows us to foster mutual respect, empathy, and love between generations.

Introduction

In-law relationships, particularly the bond between mothers-in-law and daughters-in-law, have long been the subject of scrutiny and popular culture. These relationships are complex, often influenced by societal expectations, preconceived notions, and stereotypes. In this article, we delve into the intricacies of mother-in-law and daughter-in-law relationships, examining the role of expectations and stereotypes and their impact on these vital familial connections.

Understanding Preconceived Notions and Stereotypes

Preconceived notions and stereotypes are deeply ingrained assumptions formed before we even meet an individual. In the context of in-law relationships, these notions and stereotypes are often shaped by cultural, social, and media influences. From jokes about overbearing mothers-in-law to portrayals of the daughter-in-law as a perpetual outsider, these preconceived notions can color the perceptions and experiences of both parties involved.

Mothers-in-Law: The "Monster-In-Law" Stereotype

One prevalent stereotype surrounding mothers-in-law is the "monster-in-law" image perpetuated in popular culture. This portrayal often depicts the mother-in-law as domineering, meddling, and resentful of her son's spouse. While there may be instances where conflicts arise, it is important to recognize that this stereotype fails to acknowledge the diversity of mother-in-law personalities and experiences. Many mothers-in-law forge supportive, nurturing relationships with their daughters-in-law, characterized by respect, love, and mutual understanding.

Daughters-in-Law: The "Outsider" Stereotype

On the other hand, daughters-in-law often face the stereotype of being the "outsider" in the family. This perception suggests that they are perpetually on the fringes, struggling to integrate into their new familial environment. While it is true that joining a new family can be an adjustment, it is crucial to challenge this stereotype and recognize that daughters-in-law bring unique perspectives, strengths, and contributions to the family dynamic. Building understanding and fostering open communication can help dispel this notion and strengthen the bond between daughters-in-law and mothers-in-law.

Expectations and the Impact on Relationships

Expectations play a significant role in shaping in-law relationships. Family members, friends, and societal norms often impose a set of preconceived expectations on mothers-in-law and daughters-in-law, placing pressure on them to fulfill specific roles. For example, mothers-in-law may feel obligated to provide advice and guidance to their daughters-in-law, while daughters-in-law may feel the need to conform to societal standards of being the perfect wife and daughter-in-law. These expectations can lead to misunderstandings, conflict, and strained relationships if not communicated and managed effectively.

Navigating Conflict and Building Strong Relationships

In-law relationships can encounter conflicts, but addressing these challenges constructively can lead to stronger bonds. Communication and empathy are vital tools in navigating differences and resolving misunderstandings. Both parties should approach conflicts with an open mind, striving to understand each other's perspectives and finding common ground. Recognizing the impact of preconceived notions and stereotypes can help foster empathy and create a more inclusive and supportive environment.

Breaking Free from Stereotypes

Challenging stereotypes and preconceived notions is a collective effort. Mothers-in-law and daughters-in-law can actively work together to defy societal expectations and create their own unique narrative. By embracing individuality, celebrating differences, and fostering mutual respect, they can establish genuine connections that go beyond the limitations of stereotypes. Open-mindedness and a willingness to learn and grow together are crucial in breaking free from the constraints of these preconceived notions.

Conclusion

In-law relationships, particularly the bond between mothers-in-law and daughters-in-law, are influenced by preconceived notions and stereotypes deeply ingrained in society. Recognizing and challenging these assumptions is essential for fostering healthy, supportive relationships. By embracing empathy, open communication, and dispelling stereotypes, mothers-in-law and daughters-in-law can build authentic connections and navigate the complexities of their relationship with understanding and respect. By doing so, they contribute to the redefinition of in-law relationships and pave the way for a more inclusive and harmonious future.

Introduction

Mother-in-law and daughter-in-law relationships have long been a subject of intrigue, often depicted in popular culture as fraught with tension and conflict. These complex relationships can be influenced by a variety of factors, but one of the most significant is the individual personalities of the individuals involved. Understanding how personalities can affect interactions is crucial in fostering healthier and more harmonious mother-in-law, daughter-in-law relationships. This article delves into the diverse array of personalities and their impact on these intricate dynamics.

Personality Types

1. The Traditionalist

The Traditionalist is deeply rooted in traditional values and customs. They may have a strong attachment to their family traditions and expect their daughter-in-law to adhere to them as well. Conflict can arise when the daughter-in-law's values or practices diverge from the Traditionalist's expectations, leading to misunderstandings and clashes.

2. The Nurturer

The Nurturer personality type thrives on caring for and nurturing others. They may be excessively involved in their children's lives, and when a daughter-in-law enters the picture, this can create a sense of competition or intrusion.

Daughter-in-laws may perceive the Nurturer as overbearing, leading to strained interactions.

3. The Protector

The Protector is fiercely loyal to their family and takes on the role of safeguarding their loved ones. This personality type may be resistant to change and may feel threatened by the daughter-in-law's presence. They may have difficulty relinquishing control and trusting the daughter-in-law to take care of their loved one, leading to tension and power struggles.

4. The Independent

The Independent personality type values autonomy and self-reliance. They may find it challenging to navigate the expectations and dynamics of a mother-in-law, daughter-in-law relationship. Daughters-in-law who are also independent may perceive the mother-in-law's involvement as meddling or intrusive, causing conflicts to arise.

5. The Peacemaker

The Peacemaker personality type seeks to avoid conflict at all costs. They prioritize harmony and may go to great lengths to keep the peace within the family. While their intentions are noble, the Peacemaker may struggle to address underlying issues or express their true feelings, resulting in unresolved tensions that can negatively impact the relationship.

Understanding and Empathy

Recognizing and understanding the various personality types at play within a mother-in-law, daughter-in-law relationship is essential for building empathy and fostering positive interactions. Each personality type brings unique strengths and vulnerabilities, and acknowledging these differences can lead to greater understanding and acceptance.

Communication Strategies

1. Active Listening

Practicing active listening can help bridge the gap between different personalities. It involves fully engaging in the conversation, seeking to understand the other person's perspective, and validating their feelings. This approach promotes mutual respect and encourages open and honest communication.

2. Setting Boundaries

Establishing clear boundaries is crucial for maintaining healthy relationships. Both the mother-in-law and daughter-in-law should have the freedom to express their needs and expectations while respecting each other's boundaries. Open dialogue regarding boundaries can prevent misunderstandings and conflicts from arising.

3. Empathy and Compassion

Developing empathy and compassion towards one another can significantly improve the dynamics between mother-in-law and daughter-in-law. By putting oneself in the other person's shoes and considering their feelings and experiences, individuals can cultivate greater understanding and find common ground.

4. Appreciating Differences

Rather than viewing differences as sources of conflict, embracing and appreciating them can lead to a more enriching relationship. Recognizing that diverse personalities bring varied perspectives and strengths to the family dynamic can foster a climate of acceptance and appreciation.

5. Seeking Mediation

In some instances, seeking the assistance of a neutral third party, such as a therapist or counselor, can be beneficial. Mediation provides a safe space for both parties to express their concerns and facilitates constructive dialogue, leading to effective conflict resolution.

Conclusion

Mother-in-law, daughter-in-law relationships are complex and multifaceted, with individual personalities playing a significant role in shaping interactions. By recognizing and understanding the different personality types at play, individuals can approach these relationships with empathy, open communication, and a willingness to appreciate and accept differences. With effort and understanding, it is possible to transform strained relationships into ones characterized by respect, harmony, and love.

Chapter 5. Communication Challenges
Discussing common communication issues and misinterpretations

Introduction

Mother-in-law and daughter-in-law relationships have long been the subject of jokes, stereotypes, and even tension. These relationships are complex and can be fraught with misunderstandings, miscommunications, and unspoken expectations. In this article, we will delve into the common communication challenges that arise in mother-in-law, daughter-in-law relationships and explore ways to address and overcome these obstacles. By understanding these challenges and finding effective communication strategies, we can foster healthier and more harmonious relationships within our families.

The Generation Gap

One of the primary communication challenges in mother-in-law, daughter-in-law relationships is the generation gap. Each woman comes from a different era, with distinct values, beliefs, and communication styles. This disparity can lead to misinterpretations and conflicts. The younger generation may perceive the older generation as outdated or intrusive, while the older generation may feel disrespected or undervalued. Bridging this gap requires empathy, patience, and a willingness to understand and appreciate each other's perspectives.

Unspoken Expectations

Another common issue is the presence of unspoken expectations. Both mothers-in-law and daughters-in-law often hold assumptions about their roles, responsibilities, and boundaries within the family dynamic. However, these expectations are rarely communicated explicitly, leading to confusion and frustration. Open and honest dialogue is essential to address these unspoken expectations and establish clear boundaries that respect the autonomy and individuality of each woman.

Stereotypes and Preconceived Notions

Mother-in-law, daughter-in-law relationships can be influenced by societal stereotypes and preconceived notions. These stereotypes often perpetuate the image of the overbearing mother-in-law or the demanding daughter-in-law. Such biases can cloud perceptions and hinder effective communication. Recognizing and challenging these stereotypes is crucial in fostering a more understanding and compassionate environment for communication to thrive.

Communication Styles and Conflict Resolution

Differences in communication styles can significantly impact interactions between mothers-in-law and daughters-in-law. Some individuals may be more direct and assertive, while others may be more indirect or avoidant in their communication approach. These differing styles can lead to misunderstandings and escalated conflicts. Building effective communication skills, such as active listening, empathy, and assertiveness, can help bridge these gaps and promote healthy dialogue and conflict resolution.

Cultural and Religious Differences

Mother-in-law, daughter-in-law relationships may also be influenced by cultural and religious disparities. Different cultural backgrounds can bring unique traditions, values, and expectations into the family unit. These differences can add complexity to communication and require sensitivity and open-mindedness from both parties. Acknowledging and appreciating diverse cultural perspectives can enhance understanding and facilitate meaningful conversations.

Emotional Intelligence and Empathy

Developing emotional intelligence and empathy is essential in navigating the complexities of mother-in-law, daughter-in-law relationships. Emotional intelligence involves recognizing and managing one's own emotions and understanding and empathizing with the emotions of others. By cultivating these skills, both mothers-in-law and daughters-in-law can foster stronger connections, validate each other's feelings, and engage in productive conversations that promote mutual understanding and respect.

Seeking Mediation and Professional Help

In some cases, the communication challenges in mother-in-law, daughter-in-law relationships may persist despite sincere efforts to address them. Seeking mediation or professional help can provide a neutral and supportive environment for both parties to express their concerns and work towards finding mutually beneficial solutions. Family therapists or relationship counselors can offer guidance and tools to improve communication and foster healthier relationships.

Conclusion

Mother-in-law, daughter-in-law relationships are often characterized by communication challenges, stemming from generational differences, unspoken expectations, stereotypes, and more. However, by recognizing and actively addressing these issues, both parties can foster more open, empathetic, and effective communication. Cultivating understanding, embracing diversity, and seeking professional guidance when needed can pave the way for stronger, more harmonious relationships within the family. Ultimately, by exploring and navigating the complexities of communication, we can create a supportive and loving environment that benefits all members of the family.

Introduction

Mother-in-law, daughter-in-law relationships have long been a subject of fascination, often depicted in popular culture as a source of tension and conflict. One of the primary catalysts for such conflicts lies in the inherent power struggles that can arise due to perceived authority and control. In this article, we delve into the complexities of these relationships and explore the underlying dynamics that contribute to these power struggles. By understanding the roots of conflict, we can hope to foster healthier and more harmonious interactions between mothers-in-law and daughters-in-law.

The Evolution of Power Dynamics

Throughout history, the roles and expectations of women within families have undergone significant changes. Traditionally, mothers-in-law held a dominant position within the family hierarchy, as they were seen as the matriarchs responsible for maintaining family traditions and values. However, with the passage of time and the rise of modern values, the power dynamics within families have shifted. Daughters-in-law now assert their independence and autonomy, challenging the authority once held by their mothers-in-law.

Perceived Authority and Control

Power struggles often emerge due to perceived authority and control. Mothers-in-law may feel entitled to assert influence and maintain a sense of control over family matters, including parenting decisions, household management, and even personal choices made by their daughters-in-law. Conversely, daughters-in-law may resist these perceived intrusions, seeking to establish their own autonomy and independence within the family unit.

Factors Influencing Power Struggles

Several factors contribute to the power struggles in mother-in-law, daughter-in-law relationships. Firstly, cultural expectations play a significant role. Societal norms, traditions, and gender roles influence how individuals perceive their roles and responsibilities within the family structure. Cultural clashes can occur when differing expectations clash with one another.

Secondly, communication breakdowns exacerbate power struggles. Misunderstandings, assumptions, and misinterpretations can lead to conflicts, as both parties struggle to effectively express their needs and concerns. Open and honest communication is crucial for building mutual understanding and resolving conflicts in a respectful manner.

Thirdly, the role of the son/husband plays a pivotal part in these dynamics. Sons may find themselves caught between the expectations of their mothers and wives, feeling torn between loyalty to their mothers and support for their spouses. This can further fuel power struggles and create a sense of imbalance within the relationship.

Mitigating Power Struggles

Creating healthy and respectful mother-in-law, daughter-in-law relationships requires proactive efforts from both parties involved. Here are some strategies to mitigate power struggles:

1. Establish Boundaries: **Clear and mutually agreed-upon boundaries can help define each person's roles and responsibilities within the family. This promotes a sense of autonomy and reduces potential conflicts arising from perceived intrusions.**

2. Cultivate Empathy and Understanding: **Both mothers-in-law and daughters-in-law should make an effort to understand each other's perspectives. Empathy can bridge the gap between generations and foster compassion, leading to more harmonious relationships.**

3. Improve Communication: **Effective communication is essential for resolving conflicts and avoiding misunderstandings. Active listening, expressing concerns without hostility, and using "I" statements can create an environment conducive to understanding and problem-solving.**

4. Appreciate Differences: **Recognize and appreciate the unique qualities and strengths each person brings to the relationship. Embracing diversity of thought and perspective can lead to a more enriching and fulfilling dynamic.**

5. Seek Mediation if Necessary: **In cases where conflicts persist or become unmanageable, seeking the assistance of a professional mediator or counselor can provide a safe space for open dialogue and conflict resolution.**

Conclusion

Power struggles within mother-in-law, daughter-in-law relationships are complex and deeply rooted in historical, cultural, and personal dynamics. By acknowledging and addressing these power imbalances, both parties can work towards building stronger, more equitable relationships. Developing empathy, practicing effective communication, and setting healthy boundaries are essential steps towards fostering understanding and reducing conflicts. By exploring the complexities of these relationships, we can contribute to a more harmonious coexistence between mothers-in-law and daughters-in-law, nurturing a supportive and loving family environment.

Introduction

The relationship between a mother-in-law and daughter-in-law is one of the most complex and delicate dynamics in a family. It is often characterized by tension, misunderstandings, and even conflict. One crucial aspect that can significantly impact this relationship is the establishment of emotional boundaries. Emotional boundaries serve as a framework for maintaining healthy and respectful interactions, enabling both parties to navigate the complexities of this unique relationship.

This article delves into the significance of emotional boundaries within mother-in-law, daughter-in-law relationships. We will explore how establishing these boundaries can foster understanding, respect, and a harmonious connection between the two individuals. By understanding the importance of emotional boundaries, we can create a foundation for building a healthier and more fulfilling relationship.

Defining Emotional Boundaries

To comprehend the role of emotional boundaries in mother-in-law, daughter-in-law relationships, we must first define what emotional boundaries are. Emotional boundaries refer to the limits we set to safeguard our emotional well-being, individuality, and personal values. These boundaries dictate the extent to which we allow others to impact our emotions, thoughts, and behaviors.

In the context of mother-in-law, daughter-in-law relationships, emotional boundaries involve recognizing and respecting each other's autonomy, privacy, and emotions. It entails acknowledging and validating each other's feelings while maintaining a healthy separation between the two individuals.

The Significance of Emotional Boundaries

1. Establishing Individuality and Autonomy

One of the primary benefits of emotional boundaries in mother-in-law, daughter-in-law relationships is the promotion of individuality and autonomy. Both individuals come from different backgrounds, possess distinct personalities, and have unique perspectives. By respecting each other's emotional boundaries, they can maintain a sense of self and freely express their opinions, beliefs, and emotions without feeling threatened or judged.

2. Managing Expectations

Mother-in-law, daughter-in-law relationships are often plagued by unrealistic expectations. Emotional boundaries can play a crucial role in managing these expectations. By setting clear boundaries, both parties can avoid overstepping and imposing their values or desires onto the other person. This helps to reduce conflict, resentment, and disappointment, allowing each individual to define their role within the relationship without feeling pressured.

3. Preserving Privacy

Respecting each other's emotional boundaries also involves preserving privacy. Both the mother-in-law and daughter-in-law need to have their personal space, intimate moments, and confidential matters. By establishing and maintaining these boundaries, both individuals can feel secure and respected, allowing for a healthy level of privacy within the relationship.

4. Enhancing Communication

Effective communication is the foundation of any healthy relationship. Emotional boundaries encourage open and honest communication between the mother-in-law and daughter-in-law. By understanding and respecting each other's emotional limits, both individuals can express their thoughts and feelings without fear of judgment or dismissal. This fosters a safe environment for productive discussions, conflict resolution, and the building of a stronger emotional connection.

Strategies for Establishing Emotional Boundaries

1. Open and Respectful Dialogue

Establishing emotional boundaries requires open and respectful dialogue between the mother-in-law and daughter-in-law. Both parties need to express their expectations, concerns, and limitations openly, while actively listening to each other without judgment or defensiveness. Engaging in regular conversations can help set a foundation for mutual understanding and respect.

2. Clear Communication of Expectations

Clear communication of expectations is crucial in setting emotional boundaries. Both individuals should communicate their needs, desires, and limitations explicitly, ensuring that both parties are aware of and understand each other's boundaries. This allows for the creation of realistic expectations and reduces the likelihood of misunderstandings or unintentional overstepping.

3. Practice Empathy and Understanding

Empathy and understanding are essential in mother-in-law, daughter-in-law relationships. Both individuals should strive to put themselves in each other's shoes, acknowledging the challenges and emotions that each may experience. By practicing empathy, they can foster a deeper connection and create an environment where emotional boundaries are valued and upheld.

4. Establishing Rituals and Traditions

Creating rituals and traditions unique to the mother-in-law and daughter-in-law relationship can be instrumental in fostering emotional boundaries. These activities can be regular, such as weekly tea time or monthly outings, or they can be occasional, like celebrating birthdays or anniversaries together. The key is that these rituals and traditions are exclusive to their relationship and serve as a reminder of their unique connection. These rituals can help define the roles and expectations within the relationship while providing a sense of belonging and togetherness. By establishing these traditions, both parties can find common ground and build shared experiences that strengthen their bond.

Conclusion

Mother-in-law, daughter-in-law relationships can be complex and challenging, but by understanding and establishing emotional boundaries, both individuals can pave the way for a healthier and more fulfilling connection.

Emotional boundaries provide the necessary framework for maintaining individuality, managing expectations, preserving privacy, and enhancing communication. By engaging in open and respectful dialogue, communicating expectations clearly, practicing empathy, and establishing rituals, both the mother-in-law and daughter-in-law can navigate the complexities of their relationship with greater ease and mutual understanding.

By recognizing the importance of emotional boundaries and actively working towards their establishment, we can transform this intricate relationship into one characterized by respect, love, and harmony.

Introduction

Mother-in-law and daughter-in-law relationships are often characterized by their complexities, as two individuals from different backgrounds and generations come together through marriage. One of the primary sources of tension in these relationships arises from clashes in traditions, values, and beliefs. The dynamics between the two women, shaped by their upbringing, cultural heritage, and personal experiences, can lead to misunderstandings and conflicts. In this article, we will explore the challenges faced in navigating these clashes and offer insights into fostering understanding, harmony, and mutual respect.

Understanding the Context

To effectively address clashes in traditions, values, and beliefs, it is crucial to understand the context in which they arise. Both mother-in-law and daughter-in-law bring their unique backgrounds, shaped by their respective families, cultures, and traditions. These differences may manifest in various ways, such as distinct customs, religious practices, communication styles, and expectations regarding gender roles. Recognizing and appreciating these differences is a fundamental step towards resolving conflicts and building stronger relationships.

Cultivating Empathy and Open-mindedness

Empathy serves as a foundation for bridging the gap between two individuals with differing traditions and values. Both the mother-in-law and daughter-in-law should make an effort to understand each other's perspectives, acknowledging the influence of their respective upbringings. Engaging in open and honest conversations, without judgment or preconceived notions, can foster empathy and create a space for mutual understanding.

Communication and Active Listening

Effective communication is essential for addressing clashes in traditions, values, and beliefs. Clear and respectful dialogue allows both parties to express their thoughts, concerns, and expectations. Active listening, wherein both individuals give undivided attention to each other's viewpoints, is equally important. By actively listening, one can gain deeper insights into the other person's values and beliefs, thereby facilitating constructive dialogue and reducing misunderstandings.

Compromise and Flexibility

When confronted with clashes in traditions and values, it is essential for both the mother-in-law and daughter-in-law to find common ground through compromise and flexibility. Neither party should be expected to abandon their beliefs entirely, but finding ways to incorporate aspects of each other's traditions can help build a bridge between their differences. Openness to compromise fosters a sense of equality and inclusivity, reinforcing the notion that both perspectives are equally valid.

Education and Awareness

Another valuable approach to addressing clashes in traditions and values is to educate oneself about each other's cultures, traditions, and beliefs. By proactively learning about the customs and practices that shape one's identity, individuals can develop a greater appreciation for their partner's background. This awareness not only helps in understanding the reasoning behind certain beliefs but also paves the way for meaningful conversations that promote acceptance and respect.

Resolving Conflicts Amicably

Conflicts are inevitable in any relationship, but the key lies in how they are resolved. It is crucial to approach conflicts with a focus on finding common ground rather than trying to prove oneself right. Mutual respect should be the guiding principle when addressing differences, allowing both the mother-in-law and daughter-in-law to express their feelings without diminishing the other's viewpoint. Seeking the assistance of a neutral third party, such as a family counselor or mediator, can provide valuable guidance in resolving conflicts and rebuilding strained relationships.

Building New Traditions

In the spirit of harmony and unity, creating new traditions can serve as a powerful way to address clashes in traditions and values. By combining elements from both families' customs, the mother-in-law and daughter-in-law can establish unique rituals that celebrate their shared values and promote a sense of togetherness. These new traditions not only honor both sides but also help create lasting bonds and memories that transcend cultural differences.

Conclusion

Navigating clashes in traditions, values, and beliefs within mother-in-law and daughter-in-law relationships requires empathy, open-mindedness, effective communication, compromise, education, and a commitment to resolving conflicts amicably. By actively engaging in understanding and appreciating each other's perspectives, both parties can work towards building a harmonious and meaningful relationship. Embracing the richness of diverse traditions and values can pave the way for a stronger bond, fostering love, respect, and a shared sense of belonging.

Introduction

Mother-in-law, daughter-in-law relationships have long been a subject of fascination, with their unique dynamics often depicted in literature, movies, and popular culture. These relationships can be complex, fraught with tensions and misunderstandings. While much attention is given to the roles and challenges faced by mothers-in-law and daughters-in-law, the role of the husband, as a mediator between the two, is equally important yet often overlooked. In this article, we will explore the vital role that husbands play in facilitating harmonious relationships between their mothers and wives, and examine the challenges they face in this delicate balancing act.

Understanding the Husband's Role

Traditionally, husbands have been viewed as the bridge between their mothers and wives, responsible for maintaining peace and harmony within the family. They are expected to serve as mediators, empathetic listeners, and problem solvers in the face of conflicts. The husband's role encompasses facilitating open communication, offering emotional support, and ensuring fair treatment for both parties involved. A husband acts as a critical link, providing a sense of stability and unity within the family unit.

Facilitating Communication

Effective communication is at the heart of any healthy relationship. Husbands play a pivotal role in encouraging open dialogue between their mothers and wives, fostering an environment where concerns, grievances, and expectations can be shared honestly. By actively listening to both parties' perspectives, the husband can help bridge the gaps in understanding and mediate conflicts before they escalate.

Promoting Empathy and Understanding

One of the significant challenges in mother-in-law, daughter-in-law relationships is the lack of empathy and understanding between the two parties. Husbands can contribute to the resolution of conflicts by encouraging empathy, compassion, and mutual respect. By helping each party recognize and appreciate the other's perspective, husbands can foster an atmosphere of understanding, leading to improved relationships.

Balancing Loyalties

Husbands often find themselves caught in the middle of conflicting loyalties between their mothers and wives. Striking the right balance requires tact, diplomacy, and the ability to navigate sensitive situations. It is crucial for husbands to express their love and respect for both their mothers and wives while setting clear boundaries and expectations. A husband's role is to ensure that no party feels neglected or marginalized, thus safeguarding the overall family harmony.

Challenges Faced by Husbands

Navigating the complexities of mother-in-law, daughter-in-law relationships can be emotionally and mentally demanding for husbands. Let's explore some of the challenges they may encounter:

Strained Loyalties

Husbands may find themselves torn between the expectations of their mothers and wives, leading to feelings of guilt, pressure, and indecisiveness. Striking a balance between loyalty to their birth family and their new family can be emotionally taxing, particularly when conflicts arise.

Mediating Differences

Conflicts and differences of opinion are bound to occur in any relationship. Husbands often bear the responsibility of mediating such disputes, finding common ground, and seeking resolutions that satisfy both parties. However, this role can become overwhelming and exhausting, requiring patience, diplomacy, and strong communication skills.

Emotional Burden

As the mediator, husbands may become the recipients of emotional venting from both their mothers and wives. This emotional burden can take a toll on their mental well-being, especially when the conflicts persist over extended periods. It is important for husbands to seek support, maintain their emotional resilience, and practice self-care to prevent burnout.

In many cultures, specific expectations and norms are associated with mother-in-law, daughter-in-law relationships. Husbands may face the challenge of navigating these cultural nuances while fostering understanding and harmony between their mothers and wives. Striking a balance between traditional values and individual needs requires sensitivity and diplomacy.

Conclusion

The role of the husband in mother-in-law, daughter-in-law relationships is vital in ensuring a harmonious and loving family environment. By facilitating communication, promoting empathy, and balancing loyalties, husbands serve as crucial mediators. However, it is important to acknowledge and address the challenges they face in maintaining this delicate balance. Through open dialogue, understanding, and support, husbands can navigate these complexities and contribute to fostering healthy and enriching relationships between their mothers and wives. By doing so, they lay the foundation for stronger and more cohesive family units.

Introduction

Mother-in-law, daughter-in-law relationships have long been the subject of stereotypes, misconceptions, and conflicts. These complex dynamics often arise due to differing expectations, communication gaps, and emotional struggles. In this article, we delve into the significance of emotional support and understanding from both sides in nurturing healthy and harmonious relationships between mothers-in-law and daughters-in-law.

Understanding Emotional Support

Emotional support is the provision of empathy, understanding, and care that individuals offer to one another during challenging times. It encompasses the validation of emotions, active listening, and the expression of love and concern. Emotional support plays a pivotal role in strengthening relationships, fostering trust, and promoting overall well-being.

Challenges in Mother-in-Law, Daughter-in-Law Relationships

Mother-in-law, daughter-in-law relationships are often prone to conflicts due to several underlying factors. These can include:

Cultural and generational differences: **Differing values, beliefs, and expectations rooted in cultural and generational gaps can lead to misunderstandings and disagreements.**

Boundaries and autonomy: **Balancing the need for independence and autonomy with the desire to maintain familial harmony can be challenging.**

Expectations and comparisons: **Unrealistic expectations and constant comparisons can strain relationships and create feelings of inadequacy or resentment.**

Communication breakdowns: **Poor communication or lack of effective communication strategies can hinder understanding and exacerbate conflicts.**

Role transitions: **Adjusting to new roles and responsibilities, such as becoming a mother or mother-in-law, can bring about emotional challenges and uncertainties.**

The Need for Emotional Support from the Daughter-in-Law's Perspective

Daughters-in-law often require emotional support to navigate the complexities of their new roles within the family. Some specific needs include:

Validation and acceptance: **Feeling acknowledged, accepted, and valued for their unique identity and contributions can foster a sense of belonging and confidence.**

Understanding and empathy: **Emotionally supportive mother-in-laws who demonstrate understanding and** empathy create a safe space for daughters-in-law to express themselves and seek guidance.

Autonomy and respect: Encouraging autonomy and respecting boundaries empowers daughters-in-law to make decisions that align with their values and priorities.

Emotional guidance: Emotional support can involve providing guidance and advice in challenging situations, such as parenting or marital conflicts.

Building a friendship: Cultivating a friendship based on trust, shared experiences, and open communication can enhance the emotional bond between mothers-in-law and daughters-in-law.

The Need for Emotional Support from the Mother-in-Law's Perspective

Mother-in-laws also require emotional support as they navigate the evolving dynamics within the family. Some specific needs include:

Transition and adjustment: Recognizing and addressing the emotional challenges of transitioning into the role of a mother-in-law allows for a deeper understanding of the daughter-in-law's experience.

Letting go of control: Allowing daughters-in-law to make their own decisions, respecting their autonomy, and refraining from constant interference promotes mutual trust and respect.

Active listening and empathy: Actively listening to daughters-in-law's concerns, expressing empathy, and validating their emotions create a supportive environment for open communication.

Appreciation and affirmation: Expressing appreciation and acknowledging the daughter-in-law's efforts and achievements can strengthen the emotional bond and foster a positive relationship.

Seeking a mutual understanding: Engaging in open and honest conversations, seeking to understand each other's perspectives, and addressing conflicts constructively contribute to the emotional well-being of both parties.

Creating a Culture of Emotional Support

To cultivate emotional support and understanding within mother-in-law, daughter-in-law relationships, both parties can take the following steps:

Open and respectful communication: Prioritizing open and respectful communication builds trust and allows for the sharing of emotions, concerns, and expectations.

Active listening: Actively listening to one another without judgment fosters empathy and understanding.

Empathy and validation: Demonstrating empathy, understanding, and validating each other's emotions create an environment conducive to emotional support.

Establishing boundaries: Setting and respecting boundaries ensures that both parties have the space they need while maintaining a healthy relationship.

Building a shared experience: Engaging in activities together and creating shared experiences fosters emotional connection and strengthens the bond between mothers-in-law and daughters-in-law.

Conclusion

Mother-in-law, daughter-in-law relationships can be complex, but with emotional support and understanding from both sides, they have the potential to flourish into meaningful and fulfilling connections. By recognizing and meeting each other's emotional needs, mothers-in-law and daughters-in-law can create a supportive environment that promotes empathy, communication, and mutual respect. It is through these efforts that the intricate complexities of these relationships can be explored, understood, and transformed into sources of love, support, and growth.

Introduction

Mother-in-law and daughter-in-law relationships can be intricate and delicate, often prone to conflicts and disputes. These complex dynamics can arise from differences in personalities, expectations, values, and cultural backgrounds. However, conflicts should not be seen as insurmountable obstacles but rather as opportunities for growth and understanding. By implementing effective strategies, conflicts can be resolved, and relationships can be nurtured and strengthened. This article aims to explore strategies for resolving disputes and managing conflicts effectively in mother-in-law, daughter-in-law relationships, offering practical insights to help foster healthier dynamics.

Communication and Active Listening

Effective communication is the cornerstone of conflict resolution. Both mother-in-law and daughter-in-law need to develop open and honest lines of communication. It is crucial to actively listen to one another without interruption, allowing each person to express their thoughts and feelings. By genuinely understanding each other's perspectives, misinterpretations can be avoided, and empathy can be fostered.

Empathy and Understanding

Empathy plays a significant role in resolving conflicts. Both parties should strive to understand each other's emotions and experiences, recognizing that their unique backgrounds may shape their viewpoints. Empathy helps to build bridges of understanding and promotes a sense of shared humanity. By putting oneself in the other person's shoes, compassion can replace animosity, allowing for a more constructive dialogue.

Respect and Boundaries

Respect is crucial for healthy relationships. Both mother-in-law and daughter-in-law should recognize and respect each other's boundaries, personal space, and autonomy. Clear and open communication about individual needs and expectations can help establish mutually agreed-upon boundaries, reducing potential areas of conflict. Respecting each other's choices and decisions, even if they differ, can promote harmony within the relationship.

Conflict Resolution Strategies

When conflicts arise, it is essential to approach them constructively. Implementing effective conflict resolution strategies can help navigate challenging situations. Some strategies include:

Active Problem Solving: Identifying the specific issue at hand and brainstorming potential solutions together can foster a collaborative approach. It is essential to focus on finding mutually beneficial outcomes rather than "winning" the argument.

Compromise and Flexibility: Recognizing that both parties may need to make compromises is crucial. Flexibility allows for a middle ground where both individuals' needs are met to some extent. By finding common ground, conflicts can be resolved more effectively.

Seeking Mediation: In cases where conflicts persist, seeking external mediation can be beneficial. A neutral third party, such as a counselor or therapist, can provide guidance and facilitate productive communication. Mediation offers an unbiased perspective and helps navigate complex emotions.

Cultivating Mutual Interests

Focusing on shared interests and activities can help strengthen the bond between mother-in-law and daughter-in-law. Identifying common hobbies or goals creates opportunities for bonding and reduces the likelihood of conflicts. By engaging in meaningful experiences together, both parties can build positive memories and foster a sense of camaraderie.

Acknowledging and Celebrating Differences

Rather than viewing differences as sources of conflict, embracing and celebrating them can lead to greater understanding and appreciation. Mother-in-law and daughter-in-law should acknowledge and respect each other's unique backgrounds, traditions, and perspectives. By embracing diversity, conflicts stemming from cultural or generational gaps can be minimized.

Self-Reflection and Personal Growth

Conflict resolution requires self-reflection and personal growth from both parties. Each individual should be willing to examine their own attitudes, biases, and behaviors. Taking responsibility for one's actions and being open to personal growth can lead to positive changes within the relationship. By actively working on oneself, individuals contribute to the overall harmony of the dynamic.

Conclusion

Mother-in-law and daughter-in-law relationships can be challenging, but with effective conflict resolution strategies, they can evolve into supportive and fulfilling connections. The key lies in open communication, empathy, respect, and a willingness to find common ground. By implementing the strategies discussed in this article, both parties can resolve conflicts, nurture understanding, and foster stronger relationships. With dedication and effort, the complexities of mother-in-law, daughter-in-law relationships can be transformed into opportunities for growth, love, and mutual respect.

Chapter 12. Building Empathy and Understanding
Exploring techniques to foster empathy and understanding

Introduction

Mother-in-law and daughter-in-law relationships can be complex and challenging. These relationships are often portrayed negatively in popular culture, leading to misunderstandings and tensions between the two parties involved. However, with the right techniques and a willingness to foster empathy and understanding, these relationships can evolve into harmonious and supportive bonds. In this article, we will explore various techniques to build empathy and understanding between mothers-in-law and daughters-in-law, emphasizing the importance of effective communication, active listening, setting boundaries, and finding common ground.

Effective Communication

One of the fundamental pillars for building empathy and understanding in any relationship is effective communication. It is essential for both parties to express their thoughts, feelings, and expectations openly and honestly. When engaging in conversations, it is crucial to choose words carefully, keeping in mind the potential impact they may have on the other person.

Using "I" statements instead of "you" statements can help minimize defensiveness and promote understanding. For example, saying, "I feel upset when I think you don't value my opinion" instead of "You never listen to me" invites a more empathetic response and encourages dialogue rather than confrontation.

Active Listening

Active listening is another crucial component of fostering empathy and understanding. It involves fully engaging with the other person's perspective, thoughts, and emotions. When actively listening, one should focus on the speaker, maintain eye contact, and show genuine interest in their words. Additionally, paraphrasing what the other person has said and reflecting it back to them demonstrates understanding and encourages further discussion.

Both mothers-in-law and daughters-in-law should strive to listen to each other without interrupting or rushing to judgment. By giving each other space to express themselves fully, they can create an environment where empathy and understanding can flourish.

Setting Boundaries

Clear and respectful boundaries are vital for maintaining healthy relationships between mothers-in-law and daughters-in-law. Each individual should communicate their needs and expectations openly, allowing both parties to establish mutually agreed-upon boundaries. These boundaries should be flexible and adaptable, as circumstances and dynamics may change over time.

Setting boundaries can help prevent misunderstandings, reduce conflicts, and foster empathy by establishing a framework within which both parties can operate comfortably. It is important to remember that boundaries are not meant to be restrictive or controlling but rather to ensure that both individuals feel respected and understood.

Finding Common Ground

Finding common ground can be a powerful tool in building empathy and understanding. Despite their differences, mothers-in-law and daughters-in-law often share common goals, values, and interests. By identifying and focusing on these shared aspects, they can build a foundation of understanding and connection.

Engaging in activities together, such as cooking, gardening, or pursuing a shared hobby, can provide opportunities to bond and create positive experiences. By experiencing joy and accomplishment together, mothers-in-law and daughters-in-law can strengthen their relationship and develop a deeper understanding of each other's perspectives.

Cultivating Empathy

Empathy, the ability to understand and share the feelings of another, plays a pivotal role in fostering understanding between mothers-in-law and daughters-in-law. Cultivating empathy requires individuals to step into each other's shoes, recognizing and validating their emotions, even when they may not agree with them.

To develop empathy, it is helpful to engage in perspective-taking exercises. This involves imagining oneself in the other person's position, considering their background, experiences, and emotions. By consciously practicing empathy, both parties can bridge the gap of understanding and create a more compassionate and harmonious relationship.

Conflict Resolution and Mediation

Conflicts are a natural part of any relationship, including mother-in-law and daughter-in-law dynamics. It is important to address conflicts in a constructive and respectful manner, without allowing them to escalate or fester. When conflicts arise, both parties should approach them with the intention of finding a solution rather than winning an argument.

If communication becomes difficult or conflicts seem insurmountable, seeking the assistance of a mediator, such as a therapist or counselor, can be immensely beneficial. Mediation provides a neutral space for both parties to express their concerns and perspectives, and it can help facilitate productive dialogue and resolution.

Conclusion

Building empathy and understanding between mothers-in-law and daughters-in-law requires effort, patience, and a genuine desire for connection. By employing techniques such as effective communication, active listening, setting boundaries, finding common ground, cultivating empathy, and seeking conflict resolution, these complex relationships can evolve into mutually respectful and supportive bonds.

It is essential to remember that empathy and understanding are cultivated over time and through ongoing practice. By embracing these techniques, mothers-in-law and daughters-in-law can lay the foundation for a relationship built on compassion, empathy, and mutual respect. With dedication and open hearts, they can navigate the complexities of their relationship and forge a connection that enriches their lives and those of their loved ones.

Introduction

Mother-in-law and daughter-in-law relationships have long been perceived as complex and challenging. The dynamics of this relationship are often influenced by cultural norms, personal experiences, and generational differences. However, by developing mutual respect and understanding, these relationships can become nurturing and fulfilling bonds.

This article aims to explore the significance of respecting each other's perspectives and choices within the context of mother-in-law, daughter-in-law relationships. By fostering mutual respect, we can create a harmonious environment that allows both parties to express themselves, grow, and strengthen their bond.

Understanding Perspectives

To develop mutual respect, it is crucial to acknowledge and understand each other's perspectives. Both mothers-in-law and daughters-in-law bring their unique life experiences, values, and beliefs to the relationship. Recognizing the differences and accepting them without judgment lays the foundation for open communication and empathy.

Cultural Influences: Cultural backgrounds often play a significant role in shaping individual perspectives. Recognizing and appreciating the diversity in cultural values and customs helps avoid misunderstandings and fosters a sense of inclusivity.

Generational Differences: Each generation has its own set of experiences, challenges, and societal expectations. By recognizing and respecting these generational differences, mothers-in-law and daughters-in-law can bridge the gap and learn from each other's insights.

Embracing Individual Choices

Respecting each other's choices is essential for fostering a healthy mother-in-law, daughter-in-law relationship. It requires acknowledging that personal preferences, goals, and aspirations may vary and that these differences should be celebrated rather than criticized or suppressed.

Autonomy and Boundaries: Both parties should recognize and respect each other's autonomy, allowing space for independent decision-making. Establishing clear boundaries ensures that individual choices are honored without infringing on personal space or creating unnecessary conflicts.

Career and Lifestyle Choices: Encouraging and supporting diverse career paths and lifestyles helps foster a positive environment. By understanding that choices differ based on personal goals and priorities, mothers-in-law and daughters-in-law can appreciate the value of individual fulfillment.

Effective Communication

Mutual respect in mother-in-law, daughter-in-law relationships heavily relies on effective communication. By cultivating healthy communication habits, both parties can express their thoughts, feelings, and concerns openly, leading to a deeper understanding and connection.

Active Listening: Actively listening to each other's perspectives enables both parties to feel heard and understood. This creates a safe space for open and honest discussions while avoiding misunderstandings or misinterpretations.

Empathy and Understanding: Empathy is essential in building bridges of understanding. By putting oneself in the other person's shoes, mothers-in-law and daughters-in-law can gain insights into each other's emotions, challenges, and aspirations, fostering a more compassionate and respectful relationship.

Cultivating Mutual Interests and Celebrating Differences

Developing mutual respect also involves finding common ground and embracing the differences that make each person unique. By engaging in activities and shared interests, mothers-in-law and daughters-in-law can create positive experiences and meaningful memories.

Shared Hobbies: Identifying and participating in activities both parties enjoy can create opportunities for bonding and shared experiences. Whether it's cooking, gardening, or engaging in creative pursuits, finding common hobbies strengthens the connection and fosters mutual respect.

Cultural Exchange: Exploring each other's cultural traditions and customs is a valuable way to celebrate diversity. Participating in events, sharing stories, and learning from one another enhances mutual respect and broadens horizons.

Conclusion

Mother-in-law, daughter-in-law relationships can be intricate and challenging, but with the cultivation of mutual respect, they can evolve into nurturing and fulfilling connections. Understanding and respecting each other's perspectives and choices are integral aspects of building a strong foundation.

By acknowledging cultural influences, embracing individual choices, practicing effective communication, and celebrating both shared interests and differences, mothers-in-law and daughters-in-law can foster a harmonious relationship. Through these efforts, they can create a safe space for open dialogue, empathy, and personal growth.

Nurturing mutual respect within mother-in-law, daughter-in-law relationships is a continuous process that requires patience, understanding, and a willingness to learn from one another. By doing so, both parties can develop a bond that enriches their lives, empowers personal growth, and strengthens the family unit.

Introduction

The dynamics between a mother-in-law and daughter-in-law have long been a subject of fascination and occasional contention. This intricate relationship can be influenced by cultural norms, individual personalities, and past experiences. While conflicts and misunderstandings may arise naturally, it is crucial to recognize the significance of fostering positive moments and connections in this bond. This article aims to explore the complexities of mother-in-law, daughter-in-law relationships and highlight the importance of reinforcing positive interactions for the betterment of these crucial family connections.

Understanding the Complexity

Mother-in-law, daughter-in-law relationships often face inherent challenges stemming from different backgrounds, values, and expectations. The transition from being the sole woman in her son's life to sharing that role with a new woman can be daunting for a mother-in-law. On the other hand, a daughter-in-law may feel the pressure of fitting into an established family unit while maintaining her independence and identity.

Overcoming Stereotypes

Mother-in-law, daughter-in-law relationships have been riddled with stereotypes perpetuated by media and societal narratives. The overbearing mother-in-law or the critical daughter-in-law often become ingrained archetypes, making it challenging to approach these relationships with an open mind. However, recognizing and challenging these stereotypes is vital for building a healthy and harmonious bond.

Empathy and Perspective

Empathy serves as a powerful tool in building positive connections. Both parties must strive to understand each other's perspectives and acknowledge the inherent differences that arise from generational gaps and unique life experiences. Developing empathy enables each woman to view the relationship from the other's vantage point, promoting understanding and fostering mutual respect.

Communication and Active Listening

Clear and open communication is the foundation of any healthy relationship. In mother-in-law, daughter-in-law dynamics, it is essential to establish channels for effective dialogue. Active listening, without judgment or interruption, is equally vital to encourage open conversation. By creating a safe space for both parties to express their thoughts and concerns, the relationship can evolve positively.

Appreciating Similarities and Differences

Recognizing and appreciating each other's similarities and differences can help bridge the gaps between a mother-in-law and daughter-in-law. While they may have different approaches to various aspects of life, finding common ground and celebrating the uniqueness of each individual fosters a sense of acceptance and unity. This shared appreciation can create positive interactions and strengthen the bond.

Developing Boundaries

Establishing healthy boundaries is crucial for maintaining a balanced relationship. Both the mother-in-law and daughter-in-law should be mindful of each other's personal space, opinions, and preferences. By respecting these boundaries, conflicts can be minimized, and a sense of trust can be cultivated.

Celebrating Achievements and Milestones

Another effective way to reinforce positive interactions is by celebrating each other's achievements and milestones. Whether it's a professional success or a personal accomplishment, recognizing and appreciating these moments creates a culture of support and encouragement. By actively participating in each other's lives, both the mother-in-law and daughter-in-law can create lasting memories and deepen their connection.

Finding Common Interests

Exploring shared interests and engaging in activities together can bring the mother-in-law and daughter-in-law closer. This shared experience can help build a stronger bond based on mutual enjoyment. It could involve activities like cooking, gardening, or even pursuing a hobby together. The process of discovering and nurturing common interests can serve as a foundation for positive interactions.

Conflict Resolution and Forgiveness

Even in the healthiest relationships, conflicts may arise. It is essential to address these conflicts with a focus on understanding and resolution rather than blame and resentment. The ability to forgive and move forward is vital for maintaining positive interactions. Both parties should strive to find common ground and work towards resolving conflicts in a respectful and compassionate manner.

Conclusion

Mother-in-law, daughter-in-law relationships are complex and multifaceted, but they hold the potential for immense love, support, and growth. By reinforcing positive interactions, empathizing with one another, and actively working towards building a healthy bond, these relationships can flourish. Embracing the importance of fostering positive moments and connections ultimately benefits not only the individuals involved but also the entire family unit. By embracing understanding, compassion, and mutual respect, mothers-in-law and daughters-in-law can lay the foundation for a strong, loving, and lifelong relationship.

Introduction

Mother-in-law and daughter-in-law relationships can be both rewarding and challenging. These complex dynamics often require careful navigation and effective communication to maintain harmony within the family. One crucial aspect of fostering healthy relationships is the establishment of boundaries. Boundaries serve as the foundation for respectful interactions, allowing individuals to express their needs, maintain their individuality, and preserve their emotional well-being. In this article, we will explore the intricacies of mother-in-law and daughter-in-law relationships and provide guidance on setting healthy boundaries for all parties involved.

Understanding the Dynamics

Mother-in-law and daughter-in-law relationships are influenced by a variety of factors, including cultural norms, personal beliefs, and expectations. These dynamics can vary greatly from one family to another, making it essential to approach each relationship with an open mind and willingness to understand the perspectives of both parties.

Recognizing Individual Needs

To establish healthy boundaries, it is crucial to recognize and acknowledge the unique needs of each individual. Both mothers-in-law and daughters-in-law may have different expectations, desires, and values. Taking the time to understand and respect these differences can lay the foundation for a strong and harmonious relationship.

Effective Communication

Open and honest communication is the cornerstone of any successful relationship. When it comes to mother-in-law and daughter-in-law relationships, effective communication becomes even more critical. Clear and respectful communication allows both parties to express their thoughts, concerns, and expectations without fear of judgment or reprisal. Active listening is equally important, as it demonstrates empathy and fosters mutual understanding.

Establishing Boundaries

Self-Reflection: Begin by reflecting on your own needs, values, and boundaries. Understand what is important to you and what you are comfortable with. This self-awareness will enable you to effectively communicate your boundaries to others.

Communicate Openly: Engage in open and honest conversations with your mother-in-law or daughter-in-law about boundaries. Choose a neutral and comfortable setting where both parties can express their thoughts and feelings without distractions.

Mutual Respect: Approach these discussions with a spirit of mutual respect. Recognize that each person has the right to set boundaries and that they should be honored. Avoid blaming or criticizing one another and focus on finding common ground.

Define Expectations: Clearly articulate your expectations and desires while listening to the expectations of the other party. This process helps create a shared understanding of boundaries and avoids assumptions or misunderstandings.

Flexibility: Boundaries may evolve over time as circumstances change. Remain flexible and open to adjusting boundaries as needed. Regular check-ins can help ensure that both parties feel heard and respected.

Seek Mediation if Necessary: If conflicts persist or communication becomes difficult, consider seeking the help of a neutral third party, such as a therapist or mediator. A professional can provide guidance and facilitate productive conversations, helping to strengthen the relationship between mother-in-law and daughter-in-law.

Benefits of Healthy Boundaries

Establishing healthy boundaries in mother-in-law and daughter-in-law relationships offers numerous benefits for all parties involved:

Increased Emotional Well-being: Clear boundaries foster emotional well-being by reducing stress and anxiety. When individuals feel heard and respected, they are more likely to experience a sense of security and peace within the relationship.

Respect for Individuality: Boundaries allow individuals to maintain their individuality and autonomy. By setting boundaries, both mothers-in-law and daughters-in-law can assert their unique identities and pursue their personal goals and interests.

: **When** boundaries are effectively established and respected, relationships can grow stronger. Boundaries promote understanding, empathy, and compromise, nurturing a foundation of trust and respect.

: **Clear** boundaries can prevent misunderstandings and conflicts from arising. By openly communicating expectations and desires, both parties can work towards preventing potential sources of tension or resentment.

Conclusion

Mother-in-law and daughter-in-law relationships can be intricate and sometimes challenging, but establishing healthy boundaries can contribute to their success and longevity. By recognizing individual needs, engaging in open communication, and fostering mutual respect, both parties can set the stage for a harmonious and fulfilling relationship. Healthy boundaries not only benefit the individuals involved but also contribute to a more peaceful and loving family dynamic. Remember, establishing boundaries is a continual process that requires patience, understanding, and a willingness to adapt as circumstances evolve.

Introduction

The intricate dynamics of mother-in-law and daughter-in-law relationships have been a subject of fascination and study for centuries. The intricate web of emotions, expectations, and differing perspectives often leads to complex issues that can strain even the strongest familial bonds. In such situations, seeking professional mediation becomes an invaluable tool for resolving conflicts and fostering understanding. This article aims to explore the significance of professional mediation in navigating the complexities of mother-in-law and daughter-in-law relationships, offering insights into its benefits, process, and potential outcomes.

Understanding Complexities in Mother-in-Law, Daughter-in-Law Relationships

Mother-in-law, daughter-in-law relationships are unique and multifaceted. They involve two individuals with different backgrounds, personalities, and expectations, who are brought together through the marriage of their loved ones. Such relationships can be marred by misunderstandings, miscommunications, and conflicting beliefs, often leading to tension and discord. Issues may arise from differing approaches to child-rearing, household responsibilities, cultural differences, or simply a clash of personalities. These complexities necessitate a thoughtful and objective approach to resolve conflicts effectively.

The Role of Professional Mediation

Professional mediation offers a structured and neutral platform where conflicting parties can communicate, express their concerns, and work towards finding mutually agreeable solutions. A skilled mediator, trained in conflict resolution techniques, guides the process and facilitates constructive dialogue. In the context of mother-in-law, daughter-in-law relationships, professional mediation provides several key benefits.

1. Neutral Ground for Communication

Mediation establishes a neutral environment outside the usual family dynamics, creating a safe space for open and honest communication. The mediator ensures both parties are heard and understood, enabling a deeper appreciation of each other's perspectives. This process encourages empathy, fosters understanding, and helps build a foundation for resolving complex issues.

2. Facilitating Emotional Healing

Mother-in-law, daughter-in-law conflicts are often fueled by emotional wounds that have accumulated over time. Professional mediation acknowledges and addresses these emotions, creating opportunities for healing and reconciliation. By providing a supportive atmosphere, mediators help the parties recognize and express their emotions, leading to a more compassionate and productive dialogue.

3. Objective Problem-Solving

Mediators assist in identifying the underlying issues causing conflicts and guide the parties in formulating practical and mutually acceptable solutions. Their objective approach helps cut through the emotional noise, focus on the core problems, and find creative resolutions. Mediation encourages brainstorming and compromise, enabling both parties to have a sense of ownership over the outcomes.

4. Preservation of Relationships

One of the key goals of mediation is to preserve relationships amidst conflict. Unlike adversarial approaches, such as litigation or confrontation, mediation emphasizes collaboration and understanding. By promoting open dialogue and exploring common ground, it allows for repairing and strengthening the mother-in-law, daughter-in-law relationship, fostering long-term harmony.

The Mediation Process

Professional mediation follows a structured process that typically consists of the following steps:

Intake: The mediator gathers relevant information and sets expectations for the mediation process.

Opening Session: All participants, including the mediator, mother-in-law, and daughter-in-law, meet to establish ground rules and outline the objectives.

Individual Perspectives: Each party is given an opportunity to express their concerns, needs, and desired outcomes.

Joint Discussions: The mediator facilitates structured conversations, ensuring respectful communication and encouraging active listening.

Problem-Solving and Resolution: Parties collaboratively explore potential solutions, consider different perspectives, and work towards a mutually agreeable resolution.

Agreement: If an agreement is reached, it is documented and signed by both parties. The mediator may offer suggestions for future maintenance and support, if required.

Potential Outcomes

Professional mediation offers a range of potential outcomes for mother-in-law, daughter-in-law relationships. While each case is unique, the following are some common outcomes that can be achieved:

Improved Communication: Mediation helps develop effective communication strategies, enhancing understanding and empathy between the parties.

Conflict Resolution: Mediation provides a platform for resolving specific conflicts, allowing for the development of practical solutions that meet the needs and interests of both parties.

Strengthened Relationship: Successful mediation can lead to a stronger and more harmonious mother-in-law, daughter-in-law relationship, built on mutual respect and shared understanding.

Sustainable Agreements: Mediated agreements have a higher likelihood of long-term success since they are crafted collaboratively, taking into account the needs and aspirations of both parties.

Conclusion

The complexities inherent in mother-in-law, daughter-in-law relationships demand a thoughtful and proactive approach to resolve conflicts. Professional mediation, with its neutral and structured process, offers a powerful tool for navigating these complexities. By fostering open communication, facilitating emotional healing, and promoting objective problem-solving, mediation empowers parties to find lasting resolutions and preserve their relationships. By embracing the role of professional mediation, individuals can embark on a journey towards greater understanding, harmony, and growth in their mother-in-law, daughter-in-law relationships.

Introduction

Mother-in-law and daughter-in-law relationships can be complex and challenging. The dynamics between these two individuals can greatly impact family harmony and overall well-being. In this article, we will delve into the importance of personal growth and self-reflection as powerful tools for nurturing and improving these relationships. By fostering personal growth and encouraging self-reflection, both parties can gain insights, develop empathy, and create stronger bonds based on understanding and respect.

Understanding the Complexities

Mother-in-law and daughter-in-law relationships often carry deep-rooted emotions, societal expectations, and personal histories that can affect their interactions. By acknowledging the complexities inherent in these relationships, individuals can begin to cultivate an environment of growth and understanding.

1. Self-Awareness and Emotional Intelligence

Personal growth starts with self-awareness. Both mother-in-law and daughter-in-law should invest time in understanding their own emotions, biases, and triggers. By cultivating emotional intelligence, individuals can gain a better understanding of their own needs and reactions, enabling them to respond to challenging situations with empathy and compassion.

2. Empathy and Perspective-Taking

Empathy is a vital skill that allows individuals to understand and share the feelings of another person. It is crucial for both mother-in-law and daughter-in-law to develop empathy towards each other's experiences, perspectives, and challenges. By adopting a perspective-taking approach, individuals can begin to see situations from the other person's point of view, fostering understanding and empathy.

Encouraging Personal Growth and Self-Reflection

1. Open and Honest Communication

Communication lies at the heart of any relationship. Encourage both the mother-in-law and daughter-in-law to engage in open and honest conversations, where they can express their thoughts, feelings, and concerns without judgment. Effective communication can help bridge gaps and foster mutual understanding, leading to personal growth for both individuals.

2. Active Listening

Listening actively is an essential component of effective communication. Encourage both parties to practice active listening by fully focusing on what the other person is saying without interrupting or formulating responses prematurely. Active listening fosters empathy, validates the other person's feelings, and establishes a safe space for open dialogue.

3. Practicing Mindfulness

Mindfulness is a powerful tool for self-reflection and personal growth. Encourage both mother-in-law and daughter-in-law to incorporate mindfulness practices into their daily lives. Mindfulness helps individuals become more present and aware of their thoughts, emotions, and reactions. Through mindfulness, individuals can gain insights into their patterns of behavior and develop the ability to respond thoughtfully instead of reacting impulsively.

4. Seeking Support

Sometimes, seeking external support can be immensely beneficial. Encourage both individuals to consider professional help, such as family therapists or relationship coaches, who can guide them through the complexities of their relationship. These professionals can provide a neutral and supportive environment where both parties can explore their emotions, challenges, and personal growth goals.

Benefits of Personal Growth and Self-Reflection

1. Increased Empathy and Understanding

By engaging in personal growth and self-reflection, both the mother-in-law and daughter-in-law can develop a deeper sense of empathy towards each other. Understanding the other person's perspective and experiences can help build bridges, dissolve conflicts, and foster a sense of mutual support and understanding.

2. Enhanced Communication and Conflict Resolution

Personal growth and self-reflection equip individuals with the tools needed for effective communication and conflict resolution. By cultivating self-awareness, emotional intelligence, and active listening skills, both parties can engage in more constructive and respectful conversations. This, in turn, leads to a healthier resolution of conflicts and prevents unnecessary escalation.

3. Strengthened Bond and Family Harmony

When both the mother-in-law and daughter-in-law commit to personal growth and self-reflection, their relationship can grow stronger and more harmonious. By investing in their own growth, they demonstrate a willingness to improve the relationship, creating an environment of trust, respect, and mutual support. This, in turn, positively impacts the entire family, fostering a sense of unity and harmony.

Conclusion

Mother-in-law and daughter-in-law relationships can be challenging, but by fostering personal growth and self-reflection, these relationships can be transformed into opportunities for growth, understanding, and love. By investing in self-awareness, empathy, and effective communication, both individuals can develop a deeper connection, improve family dynamics, and pave the way for a fulfilling and harmonious relationship. Personal growth and self-reflection are powerful tools that enable individuals to overcome obstacles, bridge gaps, and create lasting bonds based on respect and understanding.

Introduction

Mother-in-law and daughter-in-law relationships have long been subject to societal stereotypes and difficulties. These complex dynamics can create tension and strain within families, impacting the overall well-being of everyone involved. However, with a commitment to understanding, open communication, and empathy, it is possible to sustain healthy relationships and foster long-term harmony. This article aims to provide practical tips and strategies for navigating the complexities of mother-in-law and daughter-in-law relationships, ultimately promoting understanding and fostering a sense of unity within the family.

Cultivating Empathy and Understanding

One of the fundamental pillars of a healthy relationship is empathy. Both the mother-in-law and daughter-in-law should make an effort to understand each other's perspectives and experiences. Recognize that each person brings unique qualities, values, and expectations to the relationship. Empathy allows us to step into each other's shoes, leading to better communication and deeper connections.

Effective Communication

Clear and open communication is vital in any relationship, especially in the context of mother-in-law and daughter-in-law dynamics. Establishing a safe space for honest conversations is crucial. Active listening, validation, and expressing emotions without judgment can help build trust and understanding. It is essential to address issues promptly rather than letting them fester and potentially escalate.

Setting Boundaries

Establishing boundaries is essential to maintaining healthy relationships. Both parties need to identify and communicate their limits, ensuring that they are respected. Boundaries can cover various aspects, such as personal space, decision-making, and involvement in each other's lives. Respecting boundaries fosters autonomy and prevents unnecessary conflicts.

Finding Common Ground

Shared interests and activities can help bridge the gap between a mother-in-law and daughter-in-law. Seek opportunities to engage in mutually enjoyable experiences, such as cooking together, going for walks, or pursuing hobbies. Discovering common ground can create opportunities for positive interactions and strengthen the bond between them.

Celebrating Differences

While finding common ground is essential, it is equally important to celebrate and respect each other's differences. Recognize that diverse backgrounds, beliefs, and perspectives can enrich the relationship. Embrace the opportunity to learn from one another and appreciate the unique qualities that each person brings to the family.

Avoiding Negative Stereotypes

Stereotypes can create preconceived notions and prejudices that negatively impact relationships. It is crucial to challenge and overcome these stereotypes by focusing on individual strengths and qualities rather than relying on generalizations. By avoiding negative stereotypes, both parties can approach the relationship with an open mind and create a more positive atmosphere.

Practicing Forgiveness

Mistakes and conflicts are inevitable in any relationship. Practicing forgiveness allows for healing and growth. Both the mother-in-law and daughter-in-law should be willing to forgive each other's past mistakes and move forward with a renewed sense of understanding. Forgiveness paves the way for a healthier and more harmonious relationship.

Seeking Mediation if Needed

In some cases, conflicts may persist despite individual efforts. During such times, seeking professional mediation can be beneficial. A neutral third party, such as a family therapist or counselor, can provide guidance and facilitate effective communication between the mother-in-law and daughter-in-law. Mediation offers an opportunity to address deep-rooted issues and find mutually agreeable solutions.

Prioritizing Self-Care

Maintaining healthy relationships requires taking care of oneself. Both the mother-in-law and daughter-in-law should prioritize self-care by engaging in activities that promote their physical, mental, and emotional well-being. When individuals are fulfilled and content, they are better equipped to navigate challenges and contribute positively to the relationship.

Conclusion

Nurturing a healthy mother-in-law and daughter-in-law relationship is an ongoing process that requires patience, understanding, and effort from both parties. By cultivating empathy, practicing effective communication, setting boundaries, celebrating differences, and finding common ground, long-term harmony can be achieved. It is essential to dispel negative stereotypes, practice forgiveness, seek mediation when necessary, and prioritize self-care to sustain a healthy relationship. With these practical tips and strategies, families can navigate the complexities of these relationships, fostering understanding, unity, and love within the family unit.

"Exploring the Complexities of Mother-in-Law, Daughter-in-Law Relationships" delves deep into the intricate dynamics of this often misunderstood relationship. Through a comprehensive analysis of various aspects, this book offers invaluable insights into the challenges and opportunities faced by both parties. Drawing on historical perspectives and societal influences, it sheds light on the cultural expectations and stereotypes that shape these relationships. By examining the impact of individual personalities, communication challenges, power struggles, emotional boundaries, and clashes in traditions, values, and beliefs, readers gain a profound understanding of the complexities involved.

With chapters dedicated to the role of the husband, the importance of emotional support, conflict resolution strategies, empathy-building techniques, and establishing healthy boundaries, this book equips readers with practical tools for sustaining harmonious relationships. It also explores the benefits of seeking professional mediation and encourages personal growth and self-reflection for long-term relationship success.

Ultimately, this book serves as a guide to navigate the intricate web of mother-in-law and daughter-in-law relationships, fostering empathy, understanding, and mutual respect for a lifetime of positive interactions.

ABOUT THE AUTHOR

Mr. C. P. Kumar is a retired Scientist 'G' from National Institute of Hydrology, Roorkee, Uttarakhand, India. He is also a Reiki Healer and Chakra Balancing practitioner (with pendulum dowsing) and offers Emotional Freedom Technique (EFT) to help individuals with emotional issues. Mr. Kumar has authored many books on technical, spiritual, and social topics.

For further details, you may visit his webpage
https://www.angelfire.com/nh/cpkumar/virgo.html